1. Came the Dawn

Came the Dawn

MARY OF NAZARETH
GOD'S MOTHER AND OURS

Came the Dawn

MARY OF NAZARETH GOD'S MOTHER AND OURS

By the Daughters of St. Paul

ST. PAUL EDITIONS

NIHIL OBSTAT:
Rev. Msgr. John G. Hogan
Censor Deputatus

IMPRIMATUR:
+ Humberto Cardinal Medeiros
Archbishop of Boston

Library of Congress Cataloging in Publication Data:
Daughters of St. Paul
Came the dawn.
(Encounter book series)
SUMMARY: Relates the life of Mary, the mother of Jesus Christ.
1. Mary, Virgin—Biography—Juvenile literature.
[1. Mary, Virgin] I. Title. II. Title: Mary of Nazareth.
BT605.2.D38 1979 232.91 [B] 79-23826

ISBN 0-8198-1402-4 cloth
ISBN 0-8198-1403-2 paper

Printed in the U.S.A. by the Daughters of St. Paul
50 St. Paul's Ave., Boston, MA 02130

The Daughters of St. Paul are an international congregation of religious women serving the Church with the communications media.

CONTENTS

WHO IS SHE?

Have you ever listened to a voice on the radio or telephone frequently, getting to know *a person without ever seeing his or her face? Isn't it amazing how we can imagine him or her in our minds? Then, unexpectedly we come across an actual photograph. And what a surprise. "I didn't think he looked like that," or "I thought she was...."*

Well, what if you had heard about some wonderful person ever since you were a child? What if someone had explained the details of her beauty, her charm, her goodness? And what if they even said that she was the most perfect creature whom God had ever made? Who could she be other than God's own Mother?

In most Catholic homes Mary is as familiar as the Christmas crib. Her rosary is seen on night tables and bed posts and most commonly in the hands of humble "pray-ers." Her statues and pictures, small and great, line the nooks of most childhoods. Who is this mystery woman *that never grows old, whose name has been the quiet, luminating force behind saints, penitents, martyrs, poets and painters since time immemorial?*

There is only one of her, and she is God's own masterpiece. When she is our "star," our inspiration," every moment of every day has meaning. She brings joy, courage, wisdom, and all of the things that really count in a person's life. Loving

Mary is a sure sign of love for her Son because she never keeps any admirers for herself. As soon as she wins them, she takes them to Christ.

Just her name sounds a symphony in every heart sensitive to the things of God.

Oh, holy Mother Mary, so much a part of the pulse and heartbeat of every age, be with us in our own troubled times. We need you very much. As we conquer space, climb to the moon, probe the mysteries of nature and science, we need you, bright, beautiful human star, to bring all these victories to the feet of your Son.

We need you to soothe injured mankind who struggles under the daily trials and challenges of life.

Never abandon us, good Mother. When it comes to the things of God, we remain always and ever children. We need a Mother. All people need you, especially those who think they need you least. Stay near. Be close as we trek down the hard road of life, and eternal bliss will be as near as you are.

Keep the light of your love shining bright—bright as the faithful morning star that sets itself securely in the eastern sky.

Love us, even when our love for you is so human, so weak. Keep the hope of heaven alive. Implant it in the hearts of children. Let them know who their Mother is, O Mary!

THE HOPE THAT WOULDN'T DIE

"Joachim, oh Joachim," the woman called to her husband. A grey-bearded man entered the room.

"Anne," he said softly, still in utter amazement about something. "I know that all parents think that their babies are the most extraordinary but, Joachim, look at her," the woman said, pointing to the cradle. "Look at your daughter. Isn't she beautiful?"

"Of course, Mother," he replied, "she *is* the most beautiful baby in the world. And she is ours, yours and mine."

"And God's," the woman added hastily. "We mustn't forget God."

"Let me pick up my daughter," Joachim said. Anne watched as her husband bent down and slowly lifted the bundle in his powerful hands. He held the baby and backed up slowly, sitting down carefully on a bench.

"You act as though she could break," his wife said with a smile. But the man did not seem to hear her. He stared into his daughter's face perhaps looking for answers to unspoken questions. He spent those moments on a search back into history. With a broad sweep of his mind's eye, he scanned the growth of the unique Hebrew nation. In fact, he went back even farther than that and viewed mankind once again in the garden of Eden, first in its original state of beauty, then tainted by disobedience and original sin.

But despite the misery that man had brought upon himself, and even though some of the consequences would remain, God had said:

> " 'I will put enmity between you and the
> woman,
> and between your offspring and her's;
> He will strike at your head,
> while you strike at his heel' "(Gn. 3:15).

Thus was born the cherished hope of a Redeemer.

With the passing of time the world had become populated, and had grown evil in its ways. It had needed purification. God had directed Noah and his family on to the ark built by Noah himself. Rain pelted the earth for forty days and forty nights. The torrents became floods which swelled over all the inhabited parts of the earth and claimed the lives of every human being except those safely tucked away in the ark. At last, the rain ceased, the water subsided, and the land gradually resumed normality. As that lone family emerged from their boat and touched their feet to solid ground, God placed a multi-colored rainbow in the sky. Never again would He destroy the world by flood!

"Let me pick up my daughter," Joachim said.

Years passed. The earth was again populated. It was hard for men to be good. After the original sin they found it painfully easy to forget God, and difficult to remember Him. That priceless promise of a Redeemer would almost have been lost if it hadn't been for a man called *Abraham*. He was from the land of Mesopotamia, and had been chosen by God to become the *father* of a nation who would belong to God alone. These *chosen people* would preserve for the world the belief in the one true God, and the hope of the Redeemer. Above all, God promised that from this Israelite nation would come the Messiah. God gave Abraham the land of Canaan, which bordered the Mediterranean Sea. Then the great Jewish patriarchs, chosen instruments of God, rose to guide their people. After Abraham came Isaac and Jacob. The little nation grew strong. God promised that as long as His people were faithful to Him their land would be free and blessed.

When a famine swept the earth, one country was not suffering want because her graineries were bulging at the seams and promised to hold out indefinitely. This was due to a wise Jewish friend of the Egyptian pharaoh, Joseph. The pharaoh loved Joseph and made him official administrator of all of Egypt. This was part of God's plan, because Joseph's fellow countrymen soon migrated there and found relief from the terrible famine. The Hebrew people were welcomed and lived in peace for many years. But as generations passed, the memory of Joseph faded, and the Jews were growing very numerous. The Egyptians did not remember why they were there. They just began to resent their presence.

Pharaoh issued a decree to kill all the male Israelite babies in an effort to halt the growing population. This, fused with further injustices, made Egyptian rule unbearable, and the Hebrews longed to be free.... In the midst of suffering they were able to recall all too well the hope of the Messiah. God listened!

Moses was chosen to deliver his people through the Red Sea and the desert into Palestine, a land "flowing with milk and honey."

Pharaoh's army took off in pursuit of the whole Jewish nation. While the Red Sea parted in two at Moses' command, the Jews crossed through to safety. The enemy followed right behind! Moses raised his arm as the last Israelite reached dry land. With that, the waters again closed and Pharaoh's army was hurled into the deep. Traveling on dry land, through the cruel desert, proved difficult too, and the Israelites, weak and human, began to complain against Moses. So God punished them with forty years of wandering in that desert. He fed them miraculously with "manna," a wafer-like food, which fell from heaven six days out of seven.

Finally, Moses brought his people to the border of the Promised Land. He died peacefully on a nearby mountain. It was Joshua, his faithful disciple, who led the successful entry into the Promised Land. The conquest of stronger pagan nations already living there was possible for the tiny Hebrew army only by a miracle. Yet, they succeeded for God was with them. The Jews settled in the long-awaited Promised Land. Their whole life, culture and very being centered around the one true God, whom they called "Yahweh."

"Yahweh" was a personal God, real, directly concerned with them, guiding them through life. But, soon enough Israel noticed that all the pagan nations surrounding them had a king. They understood that their king was "Yahweh," but they wanted a visible monarch, too. First came *Saul*, then the great king, *David*, and finally, *Solomon*, David's son.

After Solomon's death the Jewish kingdom was divided by his sons. By this time there was much unfaithfulness to *Yahweh*. Great prophets foretold the fall of the kingdom, even the coming destruction of Jerusalem—men like Jeremiah, Isaiah, Ezekiel, and others. But while they foretold with great exactness the fall of glorious Jerusalem their message was not all gloom. They gave "hints" about the expected Messiah. He would be from the line of King David, said one; born in Bethlehem, said another; His kingdom would live forever was another promise, and many, many more.

Expectation ran high for the sorry Hebrews who saw their nation crumble under the merciless heel of the enemy. From their lonely exile in Babylon the Jewish people had time to think, and the severe treatment of their captors made memories of their own country more sweet still.

Years passed, and the Hebrew nation in exile, purified of its former infidelity, was liberated by the new Babylonian king, Cyrus, who let the Jewish people return home. He even helped them rebuild their temple. It was no easy task and the remnant of Jews who returned from exile faced a staggering task. God sent the prophet *Haggai* to encourage them and bolster their spirits. *Zechariah*, another holy prophet, kept telling of the coming *messianic age*, and spoke of the Messiah as the *Prince of Peace*, the humble king, and savior of the world. How much the Jews longed for this marvelous Messiah. This cherished dream helped them keep their hands to the plow, rebuilding anew.

By 175 B.C. the Greeks had conquered Babylon with an eye set on the whole world. They tried to impose their culture on the obstinate little Jewish nation, too, but the Israelites were not about to make the same mistake again. They held fast. Fidelity to Yahweh, for them, was the only way. Many died as martyrs for what they believed—Old Testament martyrs—such as the seven Maccabees and their mother. And now, after many long years of waiting and hoping, trial and error, the Israelite nation still breathed in quiet expectation of the Savior. Every family hoped that their boy might just be the longed-for Messiah.

That brings us back to the clay-like home of Joachim and Anne, who were marveling over their baby daughter. Could they possibly think that their child might play some special role in the drama of salvation? Joachim knew the Old Testament; he knew the prophets. And wasn't it the Prophet Isaiah who had once said: "...the virgin shall be with child, and bear a son, and shall name him Immanuel" (Is. 7:14)?

A GIFT FOR THE TEMPLE

Joachim went about his routine chores totally absorbed in thought. Anne prepared supper while she absent-mindedly hummed a tune. "We will have to face the issue tonight," she said aloud to herself. "But I certainly don't have much courage when it comes to things like this."

The small family gathered for supper. Three-year-old Mary listened intently as her father thanked God for all blessings received. At the end a humble child's voice added: "Thank You for me too, dear God."

Table conversation that night centered around the day's events. Mary explained about a new game she had "invented." Anne gave her daughter a kind of half-smile. She was thinking and fretting as all good mothers do from time to time. Mary was now at the age when she should be presented at the temple. There, in an atmosphere saturated with God, she would receive until the age of fifteen or sixteen, a fine formation. But the separation for parents and child certainly would not be easy.

As 2,000 years and a completely different civilization separate Joachim and Anne's decision from our own day, it is hard for us to imagine such a thing—a three-year-old child sent to live in the temple. But this was perfectly normal to them. The life-blood of the Jewish nation centered around that temple. Temple meant not only worship, as it does for us today, but culture and learning which extended to the practical things, like sewing, cooking, and housekeeping. Mary would be prepared for her role in life as wife and mother.

Joachim added some wood to the fire. As it blazed up with a new surge of vigor, he set his little daughter gently on his knee, and the two contentedly watched for a while.

Later, father and mother talked alone.

"We are old, Joachim," the woman was saying. "I want these last few years with my daughter, to enjoy her." Tears filled her eyes as she added: "Is that too much to ask?"

The man put his arm tenderly around his wife. "It *might* be too much if God wants something different. Our daughter is the fruit of a miracle, Anne. Imagine, she was sent to a couple of old folks like us. There must be an important reason."

****

"Who's coming?" one guard asked the other.

"An old Jewish couple. On foot, too. They look as poor as the rest of 'em do."

"Yeah?" queried the other, still with his eyes closed. He budged a little, finding a more comfortable spot for his back against the tree. "Of course they're poor. They aren't living off the fat Roman Empire, like us."

"Don't slam the Empire, will you now, pal. For all of its mistakes, it's still the greatest thing on earth."

"Like you said" came the retort, " 'for all of its mistakes.' "

"Get up, will ya?"

"Since you asked me so nice...." The guard raised himself to standing position, brushed off the dust and stood erect next to his friend.

"Morning," the one greeted the strangers gruffly. "Where are you going and where are you from?"

"Good morning to you," Joachim replied with a smile. "We live in Nazareth, and according to our religion we are going to visit the temple in Jerusalem."

"Kind of a tough journey on foot?" Then without waiting for an answer to that question, the guard asked another:

"Don't you Jews go to the temple to offer some kind of a gift?"

"Yes," Joachim replied simply.

"Well, pardon me for asking, but what could you possibly have to give that is worth walking all the way to Jerusalem for?"

The old man smiled, obviously not insulted by the bluntness of the remark; he turned to his wife and then looked down at a little creature all bundled up. He picked up the child and pulled back the cloak which had covered everything but her eyes.

"This is my gift," he said softly.

****

The years passed swiftly by.

A graceful young lady, working at the loom, was developing her skill at weaving. Quietly, an older woman came from behind and whispered in her ear:

"Mary, please come into the next room for a moment." The girl smiled, fastened her needle securely and followed the woman out of the room. Somehow she just knew, and her knees seemed to turn to water. She stared at the woman, waiting to hear her message, yet afraid to hear it.

"Your mother is very ill, dear. We must leave at once for Nazareth."

"Yes," the girl replied quickly. That same "yes" was always on her lips; ready, sincere, in good as well as difficult circumstances. Not too long before, her father had died, and Mary remembered realizing at the time, the painful thought that her mother would not last long without her father. A whole lifetime of loving and self-giving had molded that couple somehow into oneness.

"This is my gift," Joachim said softly.

****

It was like she was asleep. Her eyes were closed and a brief smile lit her face as though painted on, this time eternally.

"Mother," the girl whispered. "Mother!" She leaned over and touched the cold, still face. Mary sat there quietly, mourning her mother's death. All the while she prayed.

IN THE FULLNESS OF TIME

A young man sat on the hard bench of the temple. His attention was fixed upon the Scribe reading a passage from the Sacred Scroll. The words penetrated to the very marrow of Joseph's soul. It was from the book of the great prophet, Isaiah: "...the virgin shall be with child, and bear a son, and shall name him Immanuel" (Is. 7:14).

Why did this familiar prophecy of Isaiah have such significance today? The Messiah—how long Israel had waited. If there was ever a time when the little Jewish kingdom needed that Messiah, it was now, when the oppression of cruel puppet kings was grave, when poverty stalked the land, when sin and pessimism tore the spirit of God from His people. Yes, now...now!

Then, Joseph's thoughts turned to Mary. They had always known each other. She had had a place in his life ever since who knows when. Sometimes he had just seen her pass by with the women of the temple. She always left him with the memory of her simple goodness. Mary, the daughter of Joachim and Anne, meant everything to him. And somehow it was so clear that this was what God wanted. There was no one in the world who cared more about what God wanted than Joseph. God had woven His will around the youth's life. The young man did not understand it all yet, but he knew that very soon he would.

****

It was late afternoon. The sun had left a golden sunset. Mary gazed at it and smiled. If the beauties of nature were so breathtaking, she thought, imagine the wonders of God Himself. She turned slowly away from the window. Suddenly, light flashed from everywhere. The girl fell to her knees in utter amazement. Then, as her mind cleared, she became aware of a presence other than her own. It *was* someone and he was the first to speak. The words are immortalized in the Gospel of Luke:

" 'Rejoice, O highly favored daughter! The Lord is with you. Blessed are you among women' " (Lk. 1:28).

She listened with stunned awareness as the voice continued: "Do not fear, Mary. You have found favor with God. You shall conceive and bear a son and give him the name Jesus. Great will be his dignity and he will be called Son of the Most High..." (Lk. 1:30-32).

Mary believed the heavenly being. Grace touched her heart and she saw beyond Nazareth and Palestine, beyond her own era and century, far into time. God awaited her "yes." Yet, she did

"Rejoice, O highly favored daughter! The Lord is with you."

not know how all this could happen, so in her simplicity she asked the angel, who had a ready reply:

"The Holy Spirit will come upon you and the power of the Most High will overshadow you; hence, the holy offspring to be born will be called Son of God. Know that Elizabeth your kinswoman has conceived a son in her old age; she who was thought to be sterile is now in her sixth month, for nothing is impossible with God" (Lk. 1:35-37).

The seeming contradiction was removed. God's will for her was to utter her "yes," and she did. Mary said: "I am the servant of the Lord. Let it be done to me as you say" (Lk. 1:38). The great drama of salvation was begun.

ANGEL OF MERCY

The young woman sat in silence for a long time. Over and over she rehearsed in her mind the scene which had just taken place. She measured each word spoken by Gabriel and each word of her own. It meant that the Son of God was now present and living in her. It was a miracle!

It was not long before the needs of the present moment called her to action. Elizabeth, her elderly cousin, was also expecting a child. Of course, she needed help. Mary did not hesitate. She would make the tiresome journey and stay with her relative for as long as was necessary. Joseph made the necessary arrangements. She would travel by caravan. This way was safe and economical.

Joseph did not ask for details. He did not seek to know the "whys" of Mary's hasty decision. He did not even ask her how she suddenly knew of Elizabeth's need for her. He trusted Mary completely. And this trust was soon to be tried to the maximum.

Mary, wrapped in her peasant's cloak, sat on the donkey's back. She smiled contentedly as the caravan began to move.

"I will be back very soon, Joseph," she said.

"Yes, Mary," he responded, touching her hand lightly, "I will be waiting."

****

It was a tiny town nestled in the northern kingdom of Judah. The clay house of Zachary and Elizabeth offered little in the line of luxury, but love and virtue had transformed it into a home. Elizabeth had not felt well at all that whole day. As she lay silently on a cot, trying her best to hide all discomfort, noises of varying descriptions became audible. Men shouting and animals screeching—it had to be a caravan.

Elizabeth slowly rose, slid her feet to the floor and carefully stood up. She walked to the door in time to see the caravan come to a sudden stop. Two men helped a young woman to the ground and untied her belongings.

"Thank you," she said to the caravan drivers, and then added, "Please leave everything there. We will take care of it later."

It was evening and the sun seemed to find it hard to relinquish its position in the sky. Mary gazed at the woman in the doorway. She unwrapped her cloak and pushed it away from her face.

"Elizabeth!... Elizabeth!" she called.

"Mary, can it really be you?" And Elizabeth found herself speaking words which utterly amazed her:

"...Who am I that the mother of my Lord should come to me?"

"Blest are you among women and blest is the fruit of your womb! But who am I that the mother of my Lord should come to me? The moment your greeting sounded in my ears, the baby leapt in my womb for joy. Blessed is she who trusted that the Lord's words to her would be fulfilled" (Lk. 1:42-45).

"Mother of my Lord"—this was the first time that Mary was being called by that title. The great truth filled her soul once more, but instead of making her feel proud and superior, it made her admit ever more surely that all of the credit could be given to God. The purity of her virginal life was excelled only by her humility.

Three whole months Mary stayed with Elizabeth. But then, seeing that her cousin was feeling much better, and sure of Zachary's constant devotion to her, Mary left. She was anxious to return to Nazareth. As the donkey jostled along, her mind's eye pictured Joseph and the plain little home he had built for her. She saw him in his carpenter shop working and sweating, building beautiful things with his skilled, calloused hands. He didn't mind. She knew that he didn't. Nothing was too much trouble when it was done for her.

Joseph was the kind of person who could be present in any crowd but few would notice him. He was handsome, true, but in an ordinary sort of way. His great soul, his great heart, the depth of his wisdom and goodness was hidden from the world around him. But Mary knew. Mary appreciated. He was hand-picked by God Himself to be the foster-father of the Savior of the world.

When the caravan arrived in town, the carpenter anxiously went to claim Mary. He helped her descend to the ground. The respect and awe he had for her revealed itself in the bright red color which flooded his face.

Mary and Joseph were husband and wife. Days passed happily by. Mary was forever busy cooking, mending, cleaning, baking. Joseph's business was mushrooming, too.

Mary knew that she was going to have a child and she wanted so much to share her joy with Joseph, but how could she have explained the whole incredible story to him? How would it have sounded? An angel, called Gabriel, had appeared to her announcing that she, Mary, was to be the mother of God's Son—the Messiah. Even by the wildest stretch of the imagination, who could believe that this poor carpenter's wife could give birth to a God? Mary thought it over and over. At last she concluded: "This is God's plan. He will direct it. He will tell Joseph."

One night, Joseph laid in bed for a long time. But, at last, sleep crept up on him. It was then that a glorious angel appeared to him. The angel's message was brief and crystal clear.

" 'Joseph, son of David, have no fear about taking Mary as your wife. It is by the Holy Spirit that she has conceived this child. She is to have a son and you are to name him Jesus, because he will save his people from their sins' " (Mt. 1:20-21). The dream was over. Joseph sat up and shook the sleep from his eyes. The words of the dream were still vivid. Never would he have imagined this! He rose, walked over to where his wife was sleeping. The moon's rays poked their way through the small window and touched her face. She was beautiful—a rare and singular treasure. And for some peculiar reason God had chosen him to be her protector. Tears bathed his cheeks—tears of gratitude and joy.

A CAESAR, A CENSUS, AND A CAVE

Caesar Augustus, ruler of the mighty Roman Empire, loved *power.* Many throughout history have made it their god. This man had clawed his way to the highest imperial command in the world. It could make one proud if he thought about it enough. Caesar hated generalities. To rule lands was interesting, but to rule men was far more of a challenge. He wanted details—numbers. How many human beings were under his command? He had to know, for vanity's sake! A census—an exact, detailed census—was his solution to the problem. He even decided that each family should go to their native town to register. The inconvenience, the expense inflicted on the extremely poor, mattered little to him. And so the all-knowing God made use of the folly of a conceited emperor to fulfill the Old Testament prophecies.

Mary packed a few belongings which Joseph carefully strapped to the donkey. This young couple would have to journey from Nazareth to Bethlehem, for Joseph was a descendant of the house of David. It was early morning and the damp desert chill penetrated to the bones. Joseph set Mary on his donkey. He took the reins and walked beside her. The journey was begun. It was hard and uncomfortable for Mary, but she would bite her tongue before uttering so much as one word of complaint. As the hours passed by, when she caught Joseph's eyes looking anxiously at her, she would smile and say, "Everything is fine, Joseph, just fine."

It made his heart break to think that this Queen of all queens had to be subject to such miserable poverty. "Dear God," he thought, "if only You had picked some wealthy man who could have given her what she deserves."

By late afternoon the cold air was already closing in on the weary travelers. Joseph had never been so tired in his life. He pushed one foot ahead of the other. It was sheer will power that kept him going. Mary's eyes closed even though her body was constantly jostled by the movements of the donkey. They were so hungry and cold. But both were silent. Neither wanted the other to notice that they felt any discomfort.

This was the fourth full day of traveling. At last, in the distance, the twinkling of lights, whole clusters of lights, flickering their welcome. Joseph beamed from ear to ear as he pulled the stubborn donkey along. It was a town; it was Bethlehem.

"Dear God, if only You had picked some wealthy man who could have given her what she deserves."

TALE OF A NAMELESS INNKEEPER

"No room!"

"Sorry, all filled up!"

"No...no...go away!"

Joseph turned around in disbelief. He looked at his tired, dusty wife. She smiled, but hidden in that smile was so much pain. Joseph's sensitive soul felt every bit of it and he determined to find comfortable shelter at all costs. The next inn—the very next inn—he would refuse to take "no" for an answer. Camels and donkeys were tied up everywhere. Many make-shift tents had been pitched by the sides of the streets. Little camp-fires, carefully nurtured by rugged-looking men, darted and flickered in the night winds. Joseph passed them all by. He could not bear to give Mary such uncomfortable accommodations. There was another inn just ahead.

"Mary, we will stay here tonight!" he said with determination. His loud knock had a dynamic response. A large, rough-looking man opened the door, already grumbling, but Joseph spoke quickly.

"Sir, my wife is with child and cannot travel another minute. We must stay in your lodging tonight." The grouchy innkeeper, beside himself with lack of sleep, had turned away so many unhappy travelers before them. It was just getting to be too much. He felt bad, but after all, what could he possibly do—give up his own bed? "I might as well," he muttered to himself. "I'm never in it anyway, lately." All of a sudden, his face softened. The roughness, the hardness, seemed to vanish. He was looking beyond...beyond the simple carpenter. A woman, sitting patiently on a donkey, wrapped securely in a light blue cloak, looked at him and smiled. He stared, speechless, and then moved toward her. Her eyes were sad and filled with pain.

"You must be very uncomfortable," the man said awkwardly.

"I don't mind for myself," she said, "but Joseph is so worried about me."

"Of course he is. Please come inside. The fire is warm and the food is plentiful. While you are eating, I'll have one of my boys clean out a stable and fill it with fresh straw. I'll have him build a fire, too. You deserve much more, good woman, but I have no more than that to give. Come on in."

The noise and excitement worried Joseph. So many people were so upset all because of a census. He gazed anxiously at his wife hardly aware that he was eating. The couple quickly finished their meal and made their way to the cave.

The temporary shelter had a few donkeys, sheep and cattle. Then, a woman entered the cave. She glanced at the animals and looked at the empty manger in which some fresh straw had been placed. A smile lit her face. She seemed to be enjoying a wonderful secret. She touched Joseph's arm and nodded her approval. This is where they would spend the night.

Only Mary could foresee the coming event. No human mind would be capable of making up a story as remarkable as the one about to happen.

A smile lit her face. She seemed to be enjoying a wonderful secret.

A CHILD IS BORN

The barren little town of Bethlehem was at last in slumber. Every weary traveler within its gates had found some kind of rest. The chill December winds not only slowed down, but actually faded away. All was still—very, very, very still. The stars were so bright, so clear, that they almost danced—as though they were being dangled from the heavens by long, invisible strings.

Few earthly creatures were aware of the cave, the woman and her concerned young husband. But eyes were upon them nonetheless—the eyes of the just who had died in the Lord, from Abel to the last good soul who had gone into eternity still hoping for the Savior. The great prophets and patriarchs of Israel, who had spent their lives pointing to the Messiah, looked with longing and awe to that stable. All of the numberless legions of angels watched...breathless. *Tonight...tonight!*

Joseph made sure that his wife was as comfortable as could be. Then he went outside to take care of the donkey. He unstrapped their baggage, letting it slide to the ground and then fed, watered and rubbed down the tired animal. As he stood there working, his eyes began to close and he laughed to himself, thinking of his limitations. He tied the animal to a tree trunk, and then sat down on his cloak and stared into the clear night. Everything spoke to him of God—his wife in that cave, the unborn child they desired so much. There was such a feeling of expectation inside him. As he looked up at the stars again, he sat erect and stared in surprise. One star was falling, it seemed. Closer and closer to earth it came until it stopped right over the cave where Mary was.

Then, before he could gather up his thoughts and reach a conclusion, he heard the distinct cries of a baby. It had to be coming from... Impulsively he ran toward the entrance of the cave. He stopped and stared as all of the joints of his body seemed to turn to water. There, he beheld a wonderful sight. His wife, his beautiful Mary, wrapped in her weathered blue mantle, was holding a child in her arms. Mary smiled when she saw the awestruck look on her husband's face.

Joseph drew closer. This baby was more than an ordinary child. The son of his Mary was the Son of God. Faith told him so and the carpenter fell to his knees and adored Him. It was precisely then that hosts of angelic voices filled the night air with an endless refrain of *"Glory to God in the highest, and on earth peace to men of good will."* The Savior, awaited for thousands of years, had finally come.

When something wonderful happens to someone, one of the most exciting parts of it all is telling it to someone else. That is the way human beings react to joyous situations anyway, and evidently angels are the same. They just were bustling with the incredible news, and while the main number of their forces continued to fill the sky with "Glorias," a little band of heavenly "lights" decided to inform some neighboring shepherds, who watched their sheep even though fast asleep on the hard ground.

Light splashed everywhere and blinded the startled shepherds. A voice spoke:

" 'You have nothing to fear! I come to proclaim good news to you.... This day in David's city a savior has been born to you, the Messiah and Lord' " (Lk. 2:10-11).

The vision faded and night resumed. The shepherds scrambled to their feet and looked at one another. These simple men, callous-covered and rough in their ways, didn't even think of doubting.

"Let's go and see," they said. Each picked up a choice lamb, hoisted the squirming animal to his shoulders, and began the trek over the hill to the cave. They found just what the angels had said. Those shepherds had never read about the beautiful Christmas story as we have. They knew quite little about the Old Testament prophecies and never even expected this kind of a Redeemer. It would have been much more pleasing to the oppressed Jews if the Christ were a gallant warrior, a militant Messiah. But, who would ever dream... and believe...that a helpless baby, born in a cave and lying in a manger, was their God? This called

The shepherds found just what the angels had said and they adored their Infant Messiah.

for too much faith, some might say. But the shepherds put aside their own opinions, views, hopes and dreams. They were willing and ready to accept the kind of Messiah that God had chosen to send them.

Mary looked at each of them and smiled. She beckoned them closer. Each took his turn adoring the Infant God while the heavenly choirs swelled anew and filled the night.

LOCKED IN A MOTHER'S HEART

The shepherds were gone, back to their fields, resuming their long night watch. Each was silent, wrapped in his own thoughts. Somehow the night was no longer dark and chill. And the future promised to be nothing short of glorious.

Mary and Joseph were alone with the Baby. Mary picked up her Child and pressed Him to her heart. The infant Christ slept contentedly.

Eight days after His birth, the Child officially received His name. Forty days later, Joseph uprooted his little family and made the short trip to Jerusalem, to the temple of Yahweh. If only that temple could have spoken, what a story it would have told, of the blood and sweat of numberless unknown men who had rebuilt it by hand after the long painful exile in Babylon. For all of its beauty, it instilled pain in every believing Jew. This temple was but a dim echo of that glorious temple which King Solomon had once built. Sin and infidelity had torn the first temple to the ground, and it had been utterly destroyed. But a sorry, repentant, humbled Israel built anew. And this present temple represented the belief and hopes of a nation. It waited to receive the Messiah.

Temple scribes read the inspired words of the prophets. Their voices strained to the farthest regions of the vast walls. Isaiah, Jeremiah, Micah, Zechariah, Daniel, and many others served as the mouthpieces of God, prodding men's memories, lifting them to the things above. Their messages were like so many "clues" about the Christ.

"Rejoice heartily, O daughter Zion,
shout for joy, O daughter Jerusalem!
See, your King shall come to you;
a just Savior is he" (Zech. 9:9).

The little family, clothed in ordinariness, ascended the temple steps. They walked inside that hallowed spot, alert and reverent. Joseph held the Child as they walked farther into the body of the temple. It was then that Mary became aware of the piercing glance of a very old man. He walked toward her, shakily. His face revealed a stunned awe. He said not a word but gently approached Joseph and lifted the Child from his arms. The awe changed to sheer joy; his old withered arms held the salvation of the world. His voice was raspy as he exclaimed:

" 'Now, Master, you can dismiss your servant in peace;
you have fulfilled your word.
For my eyes have witnessed your saving deed
displayed for all the peoples to see:

"Now, Master, you can dismiss your servant in peace;
you have fulfilled your word."

A revealing light to the Gentiles,
  the glory of your people Israel' "
    (Lk. 2:29-32).

This Baby was all—the center of the world, the answer for all generations to come. Now he had seen everything. He had no more desires, no more secret dreams or wishes. Now his life was complete.

Then, almost as an afterthought, Simeon turned to the Child's mother and addressed to her these mysterious words: "And you yourself shall be pierced with a sword" (Lk. 2:35). What could this possibly mean? He was speaking of the sword of sorrow, for one day Mary would witness her only Son's passion and death.

LUSTER FROM THE ORIENT

The trip back to Bethlehem was quick and easy. At this time Joseph would never attempt the four-day journey to Nazareth with his precious little Baby. Bethlehem had thinned out and was back to its normal size. The census signers had returned home, so Joseph was able to find a temporary house for his family. His carpentry trade was useful anywhere. In no time at all the townsfolk would get to know and depend upon him.

Seven miles to the north of this harmless scene was the towering, sprawling palace of Herod the Great. Proud and immoral, this man no longer understood the secrets of the spirit. Nor did he live as a man destined for eternal life. Imagine his surprise when the gates of his courtyard opened and an unusual caravan circled around and around within its walls until all were inside. Three men, clothed in lavish colors, stepped forward. They were seeking salvation. Through interpreters they made Herod understand that they had tramped across deserts and climbed mountains because they *were following a star.* Herod looked puzzled and irritated. Could they be serious? They explained further that the star was different and new: It moved as though it were alive. They believed that it would not stop until it had pointed out the newborn King of the world.

Herod's ears almost went into a point. The word "King" attached to anyone's name but his own filled him with terror. His mind was racing: death to the rival even if He be just a child. But Herod was quite careful not to let his sentiments show on his face.

His court advisers whispered that, according to the Old Testament prophecies, this was the exact time for the birth of the Christ. So Herod thought to himself: "I'm not going to waste my time looking for this king in case there really isn't any. Let them do it."

"All right," Herod said to the Magi, "continue your search and when you find the Child, please come and tell me that I, too, may worship Him."

The three great men of the Orient never expected the malice hidden deeply beneath that fervent request. They were only too happy to accommodate him.

In our day and age people are forever worrying about what the neighbors think. Well, just imagine what Joseph and Mary's neighbors thought when they saw three dark, elegant figures stroll across their front property up to the door. Each carried a sparkling gift, obviously expensive,

Herod looked puzzled and irritated.

even if viewed from afar. Each took his turn passing through the narrow entrance way.

They found a perspired laborer, sawing and fixing. They saw a neat and soft-spoken woman. They saw a lively Baby. Thus after the humble folk, the shepherds, there came the great and powerful—men who knew how to humble themselves. When they had stopped at the little house, the heavenly star disappeared. It had done its work. There, the Magi found a new star. They found Mary, the morning star, who appeared then in all her splendor. Mantled in virtue and sanctity she came forth from the shadows and, presenting the Infant Jesus, said, "This is my Son."

They left that house transformed. Those three men who had cared enough to seek out the Christ, who would not let the sleepy indifference of humanity infect them and spoil their dreams, had found the answer, the goal, the climax of their long, hard journey.

Warned by an angel not to tell Herod, the wise men "tiptoed" out of Bethlehem and returned home by another route. It is said that they spent the rest of their lives preaching the "Christmas" message.

DEATH WORE RED

Mighty Herod was pacing the floor, talking to himself. Each time he turned, his cloak swished impressively. But no one was aware of this, least of all himself.

"Where is that man?" he asked, as his face reddened in anger. It seemed as though it would be only a matter of moments until he would explode. Time passed. There were footsteps, heavy, firm, resounding on the marble floors.

A tall, husky centurian stood before his king. "Where have you been?" was the greeting he received.

"Searching the countryside as you said, Your Highness."

"For whom, may I ask?" Herod prodded coolly.

"For the three men from the Orient," came the reply.

"Ah, but of course, I quite forgot. Are they awaiting my presence?"

"Er,...a...no, Your Highness, not exactly. You see we...well, I know it sounds incredible, but we...."

"We *what!*" bellowed the king. His feigned indifference could be hidden no longer.

"We can't find them," the man muttered meekly.

The king stepped forward and stood face to face with the soldier. “You had better explain yourself very clearly!”

“People from Bethlehem saw them leave days ago. Seems that they found a quicker route back home, one that didn’t take them clear through Jerusalem again.”

Herod’s mind was racing. Why wouldn’t they come back and tell him of the outcome of their search to Bethlehem? They were thoughtful, sincere men. If their journey proved futile they would have told him or at least sent a messenger before leaving. It didn’t make sense...unless they *did* find the child-Messiah and then were informed about the kind of person Herod really was. Of course that was it. They left silently because they *had found* the Christ.

“He lives,” Herod shouted. “The Messiah lives.” Then his voice dropped to a hoarse whisper, “But not for long, not for long.” He stood pensively for a few moments, and then addressed the speechless soldier:

“I order the death of every male child in Bethlehem two years old and under. Tonight!”

“No,” the soldier shouted, “no, no!”

“Yes,” the king said. His eyes were glowing. “Yes, yes. Now get out of here and do your job! I command it!”

It was the triumph of tyranny over innocence, weakness and sanctity. King Herod abused

The Child Herod feared was snuggled in His mother's arms, while a donkey jostled them along the route to Egypt.

his power; he employed deceit and cruelty—all because he jealously feared a future rival in the newborn child.

And incredibly, the Child he feared so much was snuggled in His Mother's arms, while a donkey jostled them along the route to Egypt. An angel had warned Joseph, and the little family was safely gone before the terrible injustice had begun.

The innocent children who died that night did not die in vain. They were the first of the New Testament to give proof of the divinity of Christ—of His Messiah-ship. That is why they died. Herod thought that by killing them he had killed the Messiah.

But this terrible incident marked the climax in his reign of terror. Eaten by remorse, he died a few short years later, despised and alone.

Safely in Egypt, Joseph and Mary made the best of things. The atmosphere was so different. They were alone, exiles in a strange land of different beliefs and customs. Real physical hardships faced them, but neither complained. And when they missed Israel, Nazareth, Jerusalem's temple and Bethlehem, they would turn to little Jesus, now romping about, and say to themselves that it was worth it all.

News of Herod's death meant that the Holy Family could return home. They settled in Nazareth of Galilee, that wonderful town of their youth, so rich in memories. It was there that this whole singular drama had begun, with the sound of an angel's greeting.

LIFE AT NAZARETH

Peaceful days lay ahead, but they weren't of much interest to history books because they were not clothed in the spectacular. Mary watched with delight as her little boy went through His first "this-es" and "thats." Every day, every moment was precious because she shared them with her divine Son.

Cooking, cleaning, baking, mending and weaving were Mary's daily lot. But these ordinary tasks made her grow in grace because everything was for Him. In fact, Mary, the housewife of Nazareth, earned for herself the highest crown in heaven by leading just such an ordinary existence.

If we could fuse together all the heroic deeds of the martyrs, the zealous energies of the missionaries, the merits of the apostles—all of these are but a shadow when compared with the glory that was hers.

Humility is much talked about in every age and its meaning is understood in a variety of ways. In fact, it is something which is much more easy to talk about than to live. Sometimes the best way to understand a virtue is to see it lived by others. To look at Mary, to trace her life in the Gospel story, is to see humility personified.

What is humility? Perhaps it is easier to say what it is not. It does not consist in walking around with head tilted and loud laments about all that we wish we were. St. Francis of Assisi thought of humility as a realization of who we are and who God is. Then, in this light one does everything for Him, in joy and simplicity. It was this very virtue that made Mary feel the need to pray. Oh! And did she pray! When *she* prayed, it seemed that all heaven listened and earth stood still.

The neighbors watched her with admiration. Just everyone knew what a wonderful heart she had. She was forever slipping over to a sick friend's house with some fresh broth. And caring for the neighborhood children was just the normal procedure. The gentle lady knew what to say to old folks, to the discouraged, to the troubled, to the child all disturbed over a momentary upset.

In the evenings, after supper when the dishes were done, Joseph, Mary and Jesus would sit around the fire. Joseph would read a piece from the Scriptures and the Holy Family would talk about the beautiful lessons to be learned from God's Book, the Bible. They would talk until the fire dwindled to a few sparks. Those sparks were more faithful than any clock. And Jesus, like all children, must have looked with surprise and muttered, "I know, bedtime."

The years passed by, those beautiful, peace-filled "hidden years."

Mary watched with delight as her little boy went through His first "this-es" and "thats."

THE HEART OF MARY WITHOUT JESUS

The feast of Passover commemorated a never-to-be-forgotten episode in the great love story between God and Israel. God chose Moses to lead his suffering people out of the bondage of Egypt. The journey was long but successful and the Chosen People arrived at the Promised Land. Many generations had passed since that great event, but the feast was celebrated anew each year. It was required by law that all, twelve years of age and over, go to Jerusalem for this occasion.

Mary smiled at her young son.

"Just think, Jesus, this year You, too, will go with Your father and I to Jerusalem." It was unbelievable. As she busied herself about the house, she thought of quick "yesterdays" which separated that treasured night when she first held her Child and gazed into His beautiful face. Now the Boy was twelve years old. This year He would accompany them to Jerusalem. It would be an adventurous journey by caravan with all of their neighbors and friends. The holy celebration would take seven days, and then, the return home. And that was exactly how it happened. All went well until the journey back home.

The caravan had joggled along an entire day. The women-folk walked on one side of the curious train, talking and chattering to their hearts' content. The men were on the other side enjoying the chance to talk about work and sweat and toil. All of the children present, like youth from time immemorial, got together to talk and laugh. When this became dull, they joined either parent and contented themselves in listening to grown-up conversation. Then they would hurry on to something else, anxious, restless.

Mary never even thought a thing about it when she did not see her Son in the crowd of youngsters. Of course, He was with Joseph or some of His friends. Joseph, too, noticed that Jesus was not with him but, of course, He was with His mother. They pushed on until the sun had almost disappeared. But then, as a hazy grey covered the entire earth, the caravan pulled to a halt. Dust settled. Families all started looking for one another. After a simple supper they would rest for the night so as to be ready for the next day's travel. Everyone was finding everyone—husbands finding wives, and both finding their children.

"Mary, here I am," Joseph called, "and Jesus must be with you."

"No, He isn't, Joseph," she replied calmly. "Are you sure He is not with you?"

"No," the man exclaimed. "Why, I never even doubted...." The two began their search, from family to family. He *had* to be there in the caravan. But, why couldn't He be found? They checked with every single person. Jesus was *not* among them, and no one had even seen Him once throughout the day. Fear raced through the young couple. Trembling, they retraced their steps to Jerusalem.

For one, two and three days they searched. Rest and food were forgotten. As the crowds from the Passover feast continued to disperse, the search became more systematic. Almost as a last resort they thought of looking in the temple. Silently they entered. A strong, clear child's voice was heard. Mary stopped...and so did Joseph. It was the unmistakable voice of their Son. They would have liked to rush up to Him, to embrace Him, and kiss Him, but something mysterious held them back.

They had searched for Him frantically, believing that He, too, was searching for them. Instead, they found Him occupied with other matters, as though He had no need of them.

This holy couple had learned on previous occasions that God's will is not always so easy to take, that sometimes events which are hard to understand weave their way in and out of our human lives.

"Mary, here I am," Joseph called, "and Jesus must be with you."

Yet, after hours of worry the mother could only exclaim: "Son, why have you done this to us?"

Jesus walked toward them, calm and smiling. Seeing the concern on His mother's face, He asked with genuine simplicity: "Did you not know that I must be about my Father's business?"

This event reminded Mary that her Son was destined for a mission which would some day demand even more painful separations.

JESUS THE MASTER

Ever since the angel's first greeting which had begun Mary's role in the plan of salvation, she had made up her mind to take her place at the side of her Son. Would this lead to Tabor? Would it lead to Calvary? No matter, as long as she would be where her Son wanted her to be. She believed that He would bring salvation not only to Israel, but to the whole world. How? When? These answers were becoming more and more complete as time went on.

The public ministry of Christ began when He was about thirty years old. Mary sensed that the time was near. How she dreaded to see Him go, not for selfish reasons at all, because she would follow as best she could, but because this mother alone understood what would be asked of her only Son. She knew where the Father's will would lead.

It has often been said by those familiar with God's own book, the Bible, that Jesus of Nazareth lived His life twice. How can that be? His *first* life, so to speak, was told in detail by the prophets of the Old Testament centuries before He was even born. Mary had studied the Old Testament; she knew what awaited the Messiah.

Mary scanned the growing crowd—men, women, young, old—mostly poor and illiterate. There was a ripple of anticipation. Then, a man came from almost nowhere. He was tall and gaunt, obviously well acquainted with physical privation. His jaw was set in the firm determination of a person who knows just where he is going and what he wants to do.

She knew him. She knew him at once. The little boy so miraculously given to Elizabeth and Zachary was grown. Tempered by penance, humbled by prayer and fervent reflection, this great lover of God stepped out of the bleak desert, which was his home, to fulfill a mission. His name was John the Baptist. A man of perfection, he would do precisely what was asked of him, so much so that Jesus later said of him: "There was no greater man ever born."

"Who are you?" someone asked John.

He was quick to answer: "I am not the Christ." But they would not stop with a mere negative reply. "Then who are you—Elijah? Or one of the other prophets?" After all, they reasoned, even though the prophets had been dead for generations, by a miracle God could bring one of them back.

"No," came the reply again. "In fact, you might say that I am the voice of one crying in the desert 'Make straight the way of the Lord,' as said Isaiah the prophet."

Then a man came from almost nowhere. He was tall and gaunt....

Mary listened. She grew tense. She folded her hands and fixed her gaze on him. "Of course," she thought. Her mind closed itself in deep contemplation. She was again back in the temple, a young teen, studying the large, ancient scrolls. She remembered the "Messiah" that Isaiah had portrayed, no triumphant political leader smothered in luxury and power. His Christ, the Savior he predicted, would be a man of suffering. Why, whatever could this mean? Mary knew; she understood all too well.... Back to the present moment; back to John.

John talked to his followers about the things of God as they sat on the banks of the Jordan River. Suddenly he stopped in the middle of a sentence. His voice trailed off. He glanced up at a man who was walking toward them. The Baptist rose, pointed to the stranger and called out in a loud, powerful voice:

"Behold the Lamb of God, who takes away the sins of the world." Then John embraced Jesus and took Him to the edge of the river. As he poured water over His head, the low-flying clouds seemed to split right in two. Rays of light flashed and lit the countenance of Christ. The voice of the Father overhead thundered: "This is my beloved Son. Hear him."

MIRACLE AT A WEDDING

The nameless Jewish man and woman about to be joined forever as husband and wife were the only ones who would have dared think that their love story was different and unique. Society pages of modern newspapers would hardly have raised an eyebrow. This couple was poor. They might have been able to boast of a proud ancestry, but titles are not wealth.

Their relatives and friends began arriving for the feast two or three days in advance. The women helped to cook, bake, and prepare. The day arrived; the ceremony and feasting was begun.

Music, dancing, happy chatter filled the air. A woman, dressed in light blue, moved about, helping here and there, making sure that everyone was happy. Now and then her eyes would scan the room as though looking for someone. As time passed, and everyone was taken care of, she walked outside into the tiny courtyard and sat down on a bench alone. She gazed at the bride and groom who, though immersed in the celebration, saw no one but each other. A smile lit her face as she remembered with gratitude the husband who had shared with her their precious life with Jesus.

"Joseph," she said softly to herself, "even though you are no longer on earth, I feel your presence. Now you are enjoying the reward you deserve."

****

He was tall and handsome. His red tunic lent to the dignity of His presence, yet there was nothing about Him that would make one self-conscious or afraid. His very presence filled the place, and kindness was not something He wore upon occasion, like a wedding garment; it was rather a way of life. His face was bronzed and His frame muscular—unmistakably a man of labor. Leadership seemed instinctive to Him, and all who met Him found Him to be unforgettable. Surrounded by sturdy-looking Galilean fishermen, Jesus of Nazareth entered the room.

All eyes turned to Him. Mary, too, walked toward Him radiating joy. She pressed a kiss to His cheek. He smiled at her and whispered, "Mother." How she loved to hear Him say that. The two walked over to a bench, sat down and began to talk. It had only been a few weeks since He had left home to begin His "public life," but how hard the days had been without Him, how empty their little stucco house. Several times daily she had walked into the room that had been Joseph's and Jesus' carpenter shop. All was quiet. The memories of the two great loves of her life

Mary walked toward Him radiating joy. He smiled at her and whispered, "Mother."

filled her soul with joy, yet parting seemed to mark the destiny of her life. Then, her mind came back to Cana, to the present feast. She and Jesus resumed their conversation. But again Mary's attention wandered and Jesus asked:

"What are you thinking, Mother?"

"Son," she said anxiously, "they have no wine." It was obvious that a small ripple of confusion was beginning to spread. Mary caught it immediately. The stewards were well aware that the wine containers were empty. They turned to each other, squirming as their faces reddened. Who could have the courage to mar the joy of the wedding day by telling the couple?

"Oh, no," Mary thought to herself. She saw in that couple all of the young men and women who would ever be joined together for a lifetime of joy and struggle, helping each other toward heaven. She looked anxiously at her Son. "But what can I do?" Jesus asked softly. "My hour has not yet come." Yet He knew that there could never be a refusal for His mother. She, whose great faith was never even tainted with the least doubt, looked at her Son. In her eyes shone bright and clear the belief that He was God, Lord of heaven and earth, infinite, eternal. Why, it was nothing for Him to perform such a tiny miracle. How could He refuse such confidence!

"Fill the jars with water," Jesus said to the stewards. The men did not doubt, or exchange glances or grumble. They immediately set themselves to the task. In a few minutes all of the big stone jars were filled to the brim.

There were no extra gestures or words; Jesus was thoughtful and calm. "Now, take some to the chief steward to taste," He said. One of the men plunged a dipper into a jar and did as he was told. The chief steward, completely unaware of the whole situation, sampled the wine to make sure that it was fit for the guests. He tasted...and tasted again. Shaking his head he walked over to the groom and asked: "Why have you saved the good wine until now?"

The apostles caught the echo of his voice; so did Mary. They looked at the Master. And Mary, mother-like, put her hand on His and smiled.

"IS THIS THE CARPENTER'S SON?"

"For God so loved the world," wrote the beloved apostle John, "that he gave his only-begotten Son, that those who believe in him may not perish, but may have life everlasting" (cf. 1 Jn. 4:9).

And what did the Son do to make men believe? That which He spoke, the deeds He performed proved that He was indeed the Son of God. The rich, the poor found an attraction to this Man who sought the Father's glory. He chased the money changers and sellers from the temple declaring: "Take these things away, and do not make the house of my Father a house of business."

He walked along the sea of Galilee and chose disciples. To these fishermen, Peter, Andrew, James, and John, laboring with nets He invited quite normally, "Come follow me, and I will make you *fishers of men.*"

And they walked up and down Galilee—Jesus and His first followers—preaching the "Good News." His fame spread through Jerusalem, Decapolis, and Judea, and even beyond the Jordan. What was so different about the words that He spoke?

He said things like: "Blest are the poor in spirit; blest are the meek; blest are the merciful; blest are the clean of heart; blest are the peacemakers; blest are they who suffer persecution for justice' sake." He even said:

"Blest are you when they insult you and persecute you and utter every kind of slander against you because of me.
Be glad and rejoice, for your reward is great in heaven" (Mt. 5:11-12).

Strange, wonderful words were His, words of love, of kindness, of peace, words of justice, of self-perfection, and above all, of seeking the Father's glory.

What was so different about the things that He did? Was there anything different at all? A small group of men once went up to Jesus and said: "John the Baptist has sent us to you to ask: 'Are you he who is to come, or shall we look for another?' " Jesus stepped toward them and then gestured with a sweep of His arm at the eager crowd still growing even as He spoke: "Go and report to John what you have heard and seen," He said. "The blind see, the lame walk, the lepers are cleansed, the deaf hear, the dead rise, the poor have the gospel preached to them." John's disciples were quick to draw the obvious conclusion and they hastened to tell him their answer.

What a wonderful man was Jesus...and *more* than a man the crowds were beginning to think. When something was buzzing and about to burst into real noise it was usually the Apostle Peter who brought things to a head. Jesus could depend on that. Perhaps it was for this reason that Jesus asked: "Who do men say the Son of Man is?" It was just the right time for such a question. The sun had gone down; it was early evening. The crowd had finally dispersed for the day, and the apostles were at last alone with the Master. The informal atmosphere felt good. Voices pierced the quiet, the voices of the apostles answering His question. "Some say John the Baptist, and others, Elias, and others Jeremiah, or one of the prophets." The answers were not correct. Jesus pressed further. "But who do *you* say that I am?" Peter sprang to attention and responded: "You are the Christ, the Son of the living God" (cf. Lk. 9). That *was* the answer! Jesus was not merely man but *more* than a man; He was God.

Jesus of Nazareth, born in a stable, nurtured on the earnings of a humble carpenter, had burst the bonds of His town to emerge as "Master," the Teacher *par excellence.* The world was finding out what Mary had known all along—her Jesus was the Messiah.

"But who do you say that I am?" Jesus asked. Peter responded: "You are the Christ, the Son of the living God!"

FAITH—"IF YOU BELIEVE"

Days passed and Jesus spent every moment of them wrapped in the work He had set about to do. Mary watched the crowd, though always hidden, and from the sidelines. She saw the sea of humanity looking hungrily to her Son. They all had problems, each one. Some were tormented by sheer physical pain, others by mental stress but they never even doubted the Master's ability to cure them.

A man named Jairus pushed his way through the crowd and begged for the cure of his twelve-year-old daughter. Just then a servant of the man came with the dreaded news: "Your daughter is dead; do not trouble Him." But for Jesus, helping the creatures of His heavenly Father was no trouble at all. Jesus went to Jairus' home, touched the dead girl's hand and gave her a gift. He, the divine Giver, gave her *life*.

Mary saw her Son multiply a few loaves and fish to give five thousand people their fill. She heard Him call His friend, four days dead, from the tomb with these words: "Lazarus, come forth." And the man was restored to health. She heard Him say things like: "I am the light of the world"; "I am the Good Shepherd. I know mine and mine know me." She scanned the faces of the listeners, as any mother would, eager to see if they understood and believed. How could they help but believe!

But the reaction was far from victorious the day Jesus delivered His discourse on the Eucharist. "I am the bread of life," He said. "Unless you eat the flesh of the Son of Man, and drink His blood, you shall not have life in you." All tranquillity disappeared. The silence was split in two by angry buzzing and the bobbing of heads.

"What does He mean?" someone growled, "His flesh to eat and His blood to drink?" Peter and the apostles remained calm. They didn't understand either, but they waited for the Master to explain. The minutes ticked by. Jesus watched the growing dissatisfaction. Would He take back His word? Would He change things to suit the crowd? He began again.

"I myself am the living bread
come down from heaven.
If anyone eats this bread
he shall live forever" (Jn. 6:51).

The crowd seemed to fall apart and diminish to a mere skeletal size. The face of the Master was lined with pain as He turned to the apostles: "Do you also wish to go away?" Peter felt more than the others the anxiety of his Lord. "No, no," he wanted to shout. And with all his love he answered: "Lord, to whom shall we go? You have the words of eternal life" (Jn. 6:68).

Tears lit the eyes of Christ as He responded: "Blest are you, Simon, son of John! No mere man has revealed this to you, but my heavenly Father. I for my part declare to you, you are 'Rock,' and on this rock I will build my church..." (Mt. 16:17-18). This was an important moment in the public life of Christ. It was His definite mention of a Church, "my Church," He said. This organization would be more than just a group of people who would meet to pray; it would be the Mystical Body of Christ; it would *be* Christ, living, active, working, bringing salvation to all men until the end of time.

All trace of sadness was gone from Jesus now. He relaxed in the informal atmosphere of the small group of apostles. His mother, contented that all had ended well, went with a few of the womenfolk to find lodging with friends in the nearby town. She left quietly; that was how she did everything. In the moments of greatest triumph for her Son she beamed with delight, but always in the background. Only one time would she dare emerge and ascend to the front lines. In the very near future when her Jesus would suffer the shameful death by crucifixion, Mary would be there, front and center.

The face of the Master was lined with pain as He turned to the Apostles: "Do you also wish to go away?"

"HOSANNA TO THE KING"

The crowds that were always with Jesus filed in an orderly line on either side of the road. They spread out as far as the eye could see and waited for the Nazarene to pass by on His way to Jerusalem. He came, riding a sturdy white donkey. "Hosanna to the king," voices began to shout. "Hail, hail to the king." They strewed palm branches along the road and chanted with all their heart.

The Master accepted in humility the praise and acknowledgment of His divinity, and yet as He bumped along on the colt He could see so clearly the week's coming events—the Last Supper, the agony in the garden, and the bloody details of the crucifixion. Oh, how quickly those "hosannas" would turn into the harsh cries of "crucify Him, crucify Him."

Day followed day. Soon it was Thursday, known to history as Holy Thursday. Jesus, who did all things well, was careful of every detail, of every duty that He wanted to accomplish before He closed His earthly life. He arranged the last meal together, just He and the apostles in the upper room. "This is my body," He said, as He broke bread and handed the consecrated Eucharist to His band. Then, the wine—"This is my blood." His words rang throughout the still room. He lifted the chalice of wine and continued: "It shall be shed for you." What did this mean? Peter wondered most of all. He did not always understand what the Master had in mind, and tonight especially. Jesus was talking about His death again, and Peter felt his stomach muscles tighten.

Judas had already left on an errand of his own choosing. The meal ended; the apostles followed Jesus to the Garden of Olives. "Watch and pray," He said to them and He walked on alone for several yards. Then, as though completely unaware of all else, he dropped to His knees and pain covered His face. The whole screen of coming events flashed before His eyes, and an invisible weight seemed to crush every bit of life in Him. Blood oozed from His pores and trickled to the ground as He saw the sins of mankind—from Adam to the last man on earth—laid upon His shoulders. Sin is an infinite offense to an Infinite God. Who could pay such a price? The fitting sacrifice could be only One—His Son. "Father," Jesus whispered, "if it is your will, take this cup from me: yet not my will but yours be done" (Lk. 22:42).

The Father's answer came, as it were, through the voice of a mob. "He whom I kiss is the one," the leader whispered to the unruly group. He went straight up to Jesus, kissed Him on the cheek and said: "Master." Jesus looked into the eyes of His betrayer, one of the Twelve. "Judas," the Lord whispered, as His eyes looked through the man before Him, "would you betray the Son of Man with a kiss?" (Lk. 22:48) Judas did not answer; in fact, he didn't even listen. His mind was set and the decision had been reached. So many chances to repent...but no. He stepped back, and the men grabbed Jesus to take Him away.

Peter and John ran to His aid but they were pushed out of the way. "He is God," Peter thought to himself. "Why doesn't He do something? Why? Why?" Fear blinded him and he ran into the security of a starless night. John was right with him. Together they inched their way along, following at a distance, eyes glued on angry faces made eerie by the flicker of torches. They saw the Master, serene and somber, hands tied in front, being pushed along. His face was calm; it was obvious that He was unafraid. Jesus was taken to the High Priest for questioning and trial. A long night lay ahead.

Bystanders, curious and silent, stood around the campfire outside in the courtyard. Peter and John sat warming their hands near the fire. Neither spoke. Three different people in the course of the night, came up to Peter and said things like: "You, too, were with Jesus of Nazareth." Fear forced an answer to his lips. "I don't know the man," he retorted, each time more sharply. Then, like a long slender knife that cuts its way through anything in sight came the sound of a cock's crow. Peter remembered Jesus' words

Together they inched their way along,
following at a distance....

to him: " 'I tell you, Peter, the cock will not crow today until you have three times denied that you know me' " (Lk. 22:34).

No one else even thought about the rooster's crowing, but Peter did. He looked up on the veranda just as his Master, tired and haggard, was being pushed by. And Jesus stopped, turned and looked at him. Their eyes met and spoke a silent conversation. Remorse and shame filled Peter's whole being. He ran out of the courtyard into a nearby field and wept. He was truly sorry and would spend his life making up for his cowardice.

THE GREATEST PRICE

For most people the night that had just ended had been ordinary enough. But for a certain Galilean, it was a night without end. He had been judged by the High Priest, scoffed at by Herod and beaten by Roman soldiers. Now, He stood before Pilate for sentence.

Pilate, too, had spent a hard night. There was something about this Jesus! Pilate felt so small, so insignificant, in His presence. It was ridiculous, of course. The man was no more than a self-appointed preacher, a carpenter's son from Nazareth. That was *all.* Yet, if that *was all* He was, why did so many seek His death? The whole situation frightened the Roman Procurator. The more he tried to cover it up, brush it off, ignore it, the bigger it became, like a giant web wrapping itself around his life.

"Who are you?" Pilate blurted at last. "Are you the Christ?"

"You have said it," came the Master's humble yet confident reply. More questions followed, and Jesus answered calmly, respectfully, but always with authority. At the end Pilate said with a toss of his hands, "I find no guilt in Him." He glanced at the crowd of angry faces whose emotions were mounting to fever pitch. "Crucify Him, crucify Him," they called. The crowd was fast turning into a mob. They wanted action.

Pilate felt weak and his pulse thumped in his temples. He was afraid of them, of their ability to ruin him politically. After all, he was young...his career...his future.... He couldn't risk everything for this one man. It was too much to ask. Yet, he couldn't condemn Him either; the prisoner was innocent. There had to be some way to compromise! He called for a basin of water. The crowd stopped yelling and watched. Pilate dipped his hands into the water and called out: "I am innocent of the blood of this just man."

"Let His blood be upon us and upon our people," came a nameless voice which was soon chorused by many.

Pilate was trapped. His future or Christ; his career or Christ—which would it be? There was a pause and then, "Take Him to be crucified," he commanded in a hoarse whisper.

A woman from the crowd clutched the arm of the young man beside her. "No," she moaned softly. "No, no." John stood beside her in shocked silence. Through his mind hammered the strange words of His Master, words that told about His own passion and death. John, Peter and the other apostles had refused to listen; they had had their own plans for the Christ. Now, at last, John *saw* that in the three long years he had spent with the Master he had grasped so little of His message.

Mary and John stood quietly. They waited. In a short while a man, bloody and swollen, was pushed out onto the street by Roman soldiers. Mary clenched her hands and stood speechless but her eyes spoke of an agony known only to a mother. "Jesus," she whispered, "my Son." The soldiers placed a heavy, crude cross on the prisoner's shoulder and pushed Him in the direction of Calvary hill. Never had that hill looked so high, so impossible. The mob chanted with gloomy rhythm: "Crucify Him; crucify Him." The prisoner plodded on with steady determination. He fell once, twice, a third time. A man named Simon of Cyrene helped to carry the gruesome cross.

Mary made her way to a spot on the road to Calvary where she could see Jesus best, and waited. Closer and closer the Master came until His mother could reach out and touch His battered face. There were no words...but the prophecy of Simeon filled the touching scene: "And you yourself shall be pierced with a sword" (Lk. 2:35). The soldiers shoved her back and shouted at the prisoner to continue His lonely journey. Mary followed. She could not bear to see the cruel spikes pounded through His hands and feet, even though the dull, steady thud could easily be heard. The cross was lowered into the hole dug for it. Jesus hung suspended between heaven and earth. He was paying a debt that only a God-made-man could pay. This was why He had been born. This was why He had spent some thirty-three years on earth. He had come to die that mankind might live.

A woman stood beneath the cross, wrapped in suffering, yet composed and silent. The apostle John stood next to her. Peter stayed in the back, weeping. He could not bear to go closer, to see his Master in agony and stand there unable to help.

The soldiers were indifferent about the whole situation. They failed to see the drama, the wonder of it all. One got out dice and tossed them for the Galilean's seamless robe. The others joined in, talking loudly, laughing. They even failed to hear the Lord's promise of heaven to the Good Thief. Yet, when the dying Christ spoke to His mother all was silent.

"Woman, there is your son," Jesus said in a gesture that symbolized His consigning of mankind to her care. "There is your mother," Jesus said to John. John would take care of this holy woman for the rest of her life. Mary gazed longingly at Jesus and folded her hands in earnest prayer.

Jesus called: "My God, my God, why have you forsaken me?" (Mk. 15:34) and then, "Father, into your hands I commend my spirit" (Lk. 23:46). He bowed His head in death. Large

"Woman, there is your son."

clouds rolled in, hiding the sun and covering the earth with the appearance of night. Lightning flashed and the thunder was deafening. Everyone stood motionless and watched until nature had paid its final tribute. Then, all was quiet. A soldier plunged his spear into the side of Christ.

The God-man was dead and the world's salvation was accomplished.

VICTORY

A man named Joseph from Arimathea—quiet, wealthy, a hidden follower of Christ—obtained Pilate's permission to take the body of Jesus. He climbed up a ladder, and, with the help of a few friends, unfastened the broken body, and lowered it. A mother waited with arms stretched up. Her sobs were muffled, soundless. They laid Jesus across her lap. She lifted His face to her chest and leaned her own face on His. "Oh, my Son," she whispered again and again. Then the men lifted Jesus onto a stretcher, and the small procession went its way to a sepulcher made ready.

Mary, the beautiful mother of God, knelt for a long time there. She prayed for strength to continue in God's will, and she prayed that faith and courage be planted and made firm in the apostles. Her Son's work upon earth was not done. She knew that His desire to fill the whole world with His doctrine of salvation was for His followers to carry out. And she was anxious to see the plans unfold.

On Saturday all was very quiet. But Sunday dawned bright with victory. Jesus of Nazareth rose from the dead. He appeared to His mother; He broke bread with the apostles; He walked with the disciples to Emmaus. And for forty days He continued His task of stabilizing the Church He had founded. To the apostles, still fearful and hesitant, He promised to send the Holy Spirit to mold and strengthen them, thus making them fit for their mission.

Then, in the presence of His mother and some one hundred and twenty-five followers He was lifted up from the ground, higher and higher, until the clouds hid Him from view. His mother stared anxiously. His final words were still ringing in her ears: "Go into the whole world," He had said to the apostles, "and proclaim the good news to all creation" (Mk. 16:15). Even at that moment, Mary sensed the earnestness in the apostles and saw her mission as their teacher and guide. She stayed with them in the Upper Room until Pentecost Sunday; she witnessed the fiery tongues resting on each one's head. She saw a group of bewildered, awkward men transformed into valiant apostles athirst with love for her Son, and anxious to take His message to the ends of the earth.

She saw them leave, two by two, dividing the then known world. They weren't afraid of the odds for they were mere instruments in the hands of God. Mary followed them with her thoughts, desires, sentiments. How she longed to go with them, to spend her life for the Gospel. But her place was not there. She would go with John to Ephesus and make her home there to begin the

They began the trip back to Ephesus, a woman on a donkey guided by John, a sturdy young man.

final stage of her mission—praying and sacrificing for Christ's mystical body, the Church.

They began the trip back to Ephesus, a woman on a donkey guided by John, a sturdy young man. How insignificant these two Galileans looked. The world that passed them by looked for glitter and splash. And so, Mary of Nazareth, God's masterpiece, returned to the shadows, wrapped in obscurity.

THE ETERNAL MOTHER

Mary spent the rest of her life at Ephesus in prayer, watching the growth of her Son's mustard-seed Church. The apostles kept her informed of the conquests in "His" name and she kept the joy in her heart with that same humility that was evident in sorrows as well.

How she longed to be with Jesus, to taste paradise, her final home. After her earthly life was done, Mary was assumed body and soul into heaven where she was crowned Queen of heaven and earth. This privilege is called her "Assumption." God's perfect creature, never tainted by any sin, even from the first moment of her existence, this living tabernacle that clothed the Son of God with humanity, never knew the decay of the grave.

From paradise, where she reigns, she spends her eternity interceding for humanity before the throne of God. The words uttered by her Son some two thousand years ago as He hung from a cross are as real and clear to her today as when they were first uttered: "Woman, there is your son." In those words she saw us all—every man, woman and child who ever lived, or ever would. All are her children!

And how much we need her! She is the mother who opens doors of all kinds, clears away obstacles, gives courage to stand straight, and the humility to see and admit when we are wrong. She who never was touched by personal sin understands the sinner and takes him to her Son. She who is mother and yet ever-virgin guides vocations to the priesthood, religious life and married state. She who is the greatest of all saints knows how to guide others to holiness.

Just as Jesus chose to come to this earth through Mary, so He desires that we use this same means to find our way to heaven.

" 'Woman, there is your son....' Mother, here I am. Walk with me through life. Help me to remain your child forever and open up heaven's gates for me some day."

The Eternal Mother

GREAT HEROES OF GOD

DSP Encounter Books

A goldmine of enjoyable reading and wholesome inspiration, written in a smooth-flowing style for fourth to eighth graders (and their families). Great heroes and saints of God come alive with all the dynamism of their noble ideals. Each volume illustrated.

$3.00 cloth (unless otherwise noted); $2.00 paper (only starred titles are available in paper)

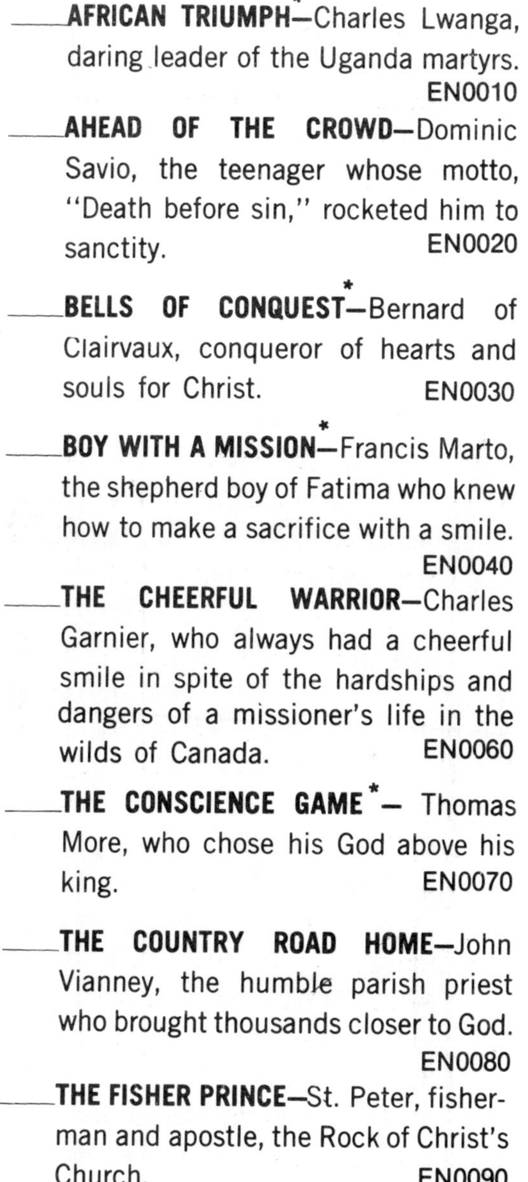

____**AFRICAN TRIUMPH**[*]—Charles Lwanga, daring leader of the Uganda martyrs. EN0010

____**AHEAD OF THE CROWD**—Dominic Savio, the teenager whose motto, "Death before sin," rocketed him to sanctity. EN0020

____**BELLS OF CONQUEST**[*]—Bernard of Clairvaux, conqueror of hearts and souls for Christ. EN0030

____**BOY WITH A MISSION**[*]—Francis Marto, the shepherd boy of Fatima who knew how to make a sacrifice with a smile. EN0040

____**THE CHEERFUL WARRIOR**—Charles Garnier, who always had a cheerful smile in spite of the hardships and dangers of a missioner's life in the wilds of Canada. EN0060

____**THE CONSCIENCE GAME**[*]— Thomas More, who chose his God above his king. EN0070

____**THE COUNTRY ROAD HOME**—John Vianney, the humble parish priest who brought thousands closer to God. EN0080

____**THE FISHER PRINCE**—St. Peter, fisherman and apostle, the Rock of Christ's Church. EN0090

____**FLAME IN THE NIGHT***—Francis Xavier, pioneer missionary to the mysterious Far East. EN0100

____**FOOTSTEPS OF A GIANT**—Charles Borromeo's tireless labor during the Council of Trent continued afterwards in fidelity to reform, to change of heart and conduct in the flock entrusted to him. EN0110

____**GIRL IN THE STABLE***—Germaine, the quiet and gentle girl who never felt sorry for herself. EN0130

____**GOD'S SECRET AGENT***—Father Michael Pro, S.J., a modern martyr and daring hero for Christ. EN0140

____**HER DREAM CAME TRUE**—Imelda, a young girl with an overpowering love for Christ in the Eucharist. EN0160

____**LIGHT IN THE GROTTO***—Bernadette, "the little nobody" who brought the world to our Lady's feet. EN0170

____**LOVE AS STRONG AS DEATH**—St. Thecla, the courageous virgin who followed Christ in spite of trial and torment. EN0180

____**MADEMOISELLE LOUISE** — Louise de Marillac—lovely, aristocratic, happy and saintly. EN0190

____**MARY'S PILGRIM**—Peregrine—from a teenage gang leader he became a leader for Christ through a powerful friendship with Mary. EN0200

____**MUSIC MASTER**—Herman Cohen, the talented musician who knew how to sacrifice all for the Lord he loved. EN0210

____**NOBLE LADY**—The gentle, valiant St. Helen who found the true cross. EN0230

____**NO PLACE FOR DEFEAT**—Pius V, the Pope who was a Dominican monk, renowned for his orthodoxy, his courage and mildness. EN0220

____**WIND AND SHADOWS***—Joan of Arc, the daring warrior-maid dedicated to her God and her nation. EN0250

____**CATHERINE OF SIENA**—The story of one of the greatest women in the history of the Catholic Church. EN0050

____**TRAILBLAZER FOR THE SACRED HEART**—The fascinating life of Father Mateo Crawley-Boevey, SS.CC., founder of the Enthronement of the Sacred Heart of Jesus in the home. His goal in life was: the whole world conquered for the Sacred Heart. $3.00 EN0245

____**GENTLE REVOLUTIONARY**—Saint Francis of Assisi, the man whose unbelievable witness of Christ-likeness rings in every page. EN0120

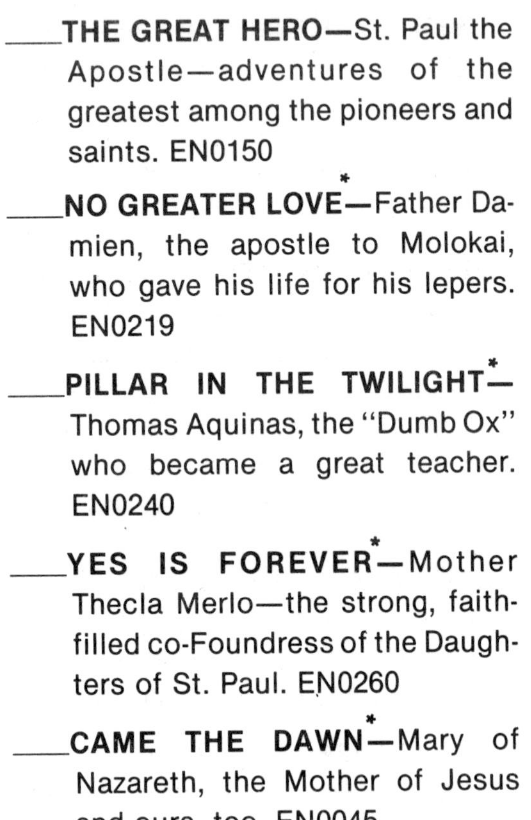

____**THE GREAT HERO**—St. Paul the Apostle—adventures of the greatest among the pioneers and saints. EN0150

____**NO GREATER LOVE***—Father Damien, the apostle to Molokai, who gave his life for his lepers. EN0219

____**PILLAR IN THE TWILIGHT***—Thomas Aquinas, the "Dumb Ox" who became a great teacher. EN0240

____**YES IS FOREVER***—Mother Thecla Merlo—the strong, faith-filled co-Foundress of the Daughters of St. Paul. EN0260

____**CAME THE DAWN***—Mary of Nazareth, the Mother of Jesus and ours, too. EN0045

Order from addresses on following page.

Please include 75¢ postage for each book and 15¢ for each additional book.

Daughters of St. Paul

IN MASSACHUSETTS
50 St. Paul's Ave., Jamaica Plain, Boston, MA 02130; **617-522-8911; 617-522-0875**
172 Tremont Street, Boston, MA 02111; **617-426-5464; 617-426-4230**
IN NEW YORK
78 Fort Place, Staten Island, NY 10301; **212-447-5071**
59 East 43rd Street, New York, NY 10017; **212-986-7580**
625 East 187th Street, Bronx, NY 10458; **212-584-0440**
525 Main Street, Buffalo, NY 14203; **716-847-6044**
IN NEW JERSEY
Hudson Mall — Route 440 and Communipaw Ave., Jersey City, NJ 07304; **201-433-7740**
IN CONNECTICUT
202 Fairfield Ave., Bridgeport, CT 06604; **203-335-9913**
IN OHIO
2105 Ontario St. (at Prospect Ave.), Cleveland, OH 44115; **216-621-9427**
25 E. Eighth Street, Cincinnati, OH 45202; **513-721-4838**
IN PENNSYLVANIA
1719 Chestnut Street, Philadelphia, PA 19103; **215-568-2638**
IN VIRGINIA
1025 King St., Alexandria, VA 22314
IN FLORIDA
2700 Biscayne Blvd., Miami, FL 33137; **305-573-1618**
IN LOUISIANA
4403 Veterans Memorial Blvd., Metairie, LA 70002; **504-887-7631; 504-887-0113**
1800 South Acadian Thruway, P.O. Box 2028, Baton Rouge, LA 70821 **504-343-4057; 504-343-3814**
IN MISSOURI
1001 Pine Street (at North 10th), St. Louis, MO 63101; **314-621-0346; 314-231-1034**
IN ILLINOIS
172 North Michigan Ave., Chicago, IL 60601; **312-346-4228 312-346-3240**
IN TEXAS
114 Main Plaza, San Antonio, TX 78205; **512-224-8101**
IN CALIFORNIA
1570 Fifth Avenue, San Diego, CA 92101; **714-232-1442**
46 Geary Street, San Francisco, CA 94108; **415-781-5180**
IN HAWAII
1143 Bishop Street, Honolulu, HI 96813; **808-521-2731**
IN ALASKA
750 West 5th Avenue, Anchorage AK 99501; **907-272-8183**
IN CANADA
3022 Dufferin Street, Toronto 395, Ontario, Canada
IN ENGLAND
128, Notting Hill Gate, London W11 3QG, England
133 Corporation Street, Birmingham B4 6PH, England
5A-7 Royal Exchange Square, Glasgow G1 3AH, England
82 Bold Street, Liverpool L1 4HR, England
IN AUSTRALIA
58 Abbotsford Rd., Homebush, N.S.W., Sydney 2140, Australia